These Now & Other Poems

Other books by Michael Blitz:

Partitions
The Spacialist
Five Days in the Electric Chair
Suction Files
Truck Drivers of the Marvelous

Also:

Composition and Resistance
(with C. Mark Hurlbert)

Letters for the Living: Teaching Writing in a Violent Age
(with C. Mark Hurlbert)

These Now & Other Poems

Michael Blitz

Writers Club Press
San Jose   New York   Lincoln   Shanghai

These Now & Other Poems

All Rights Reserved © 2002 by Michael Blitz

No part of this book may be reproduced or transmitted in any form or by any means, graphic, electronic, or mechanical, including photocopying, recording, taping, or by any information storage retrieval system, without the permission in writing from the publisher.

Writers Club Press
an imprint of iUniverse, Inc.

For information address:
iUniverse, Inc.
5220 S. 16th St., Suite 200
Lincoln, NE 68512
www.iuniverse.com

ISBN: 0-595-21552-1

Printed in the United States of America

Contents

Other Poems

Capital Letters 3
At My Father's Piano— 5
Blank Pages 7
For My Father's 70th Birthday 8
And 10
"be still my heart…" 12
Bus Accident 14
Day of Rest 18
Thoughts of Everything 19
Footnote 20
The Instructions 21
The Simple Truth: 22
Often I Am Permitted Two For One 23
this side) 24
User Friendly 27
You know that 28
No Power Is 29
Bellows 33

These Now

These Now 39

For the Going and the Gone

Other Poems

Your poems aren't like other poems. Other poems have more nature in them. Your poems are....unnatural.

[Daina Ariel Blitz, 1995]

～ Capital Letters

knowledge of your sorrows
doesn't equal sorrow
still
you know what you know and
remember the rise and wash of grief
as if grief itself was your soul
what the letters spell
is not the same
as the letter's spell
as if the rise and fall of each pen-stroke
falters in your reading of the choked
remarks
later you know again the choking
was your own
and the words on the page
lie shattered
into syllables you cannot reassemble
or
later you know again the choking on the page
was your own shattered assembly
of a soul you cannot recover
your soul and the soul you
remember
out of the nagging sadness that
spells a life

had there been a message
to which your reply
might complete a circuit
spun out of rage
the silence of which might rise

These Now & Other Poems

in the rise of your capital letters
your names for the sorrows
whose names do not equal the grief they require
had there been a time you didn't cry out of your
    dream
the same broken matters your life resembles
had you once distinguished between light and
longing
you could forget your desire to turn letters
to whispers
and words sick with wanting you have
had to cut loose from who you are.

∽ *At My Father's Piano—*

that it could be so
silent

that I could sleep through his dream,
his hands at the piano,
fitful turning
my head
leaves a dark stain

as if a conversation could end
without knowing it,
each word
wedged
between his anger, fits of terrifying laughter
and two hands hammering
the stained keys

that such music could be
heard again

I do not fit into my sleep
nor the strained key of his music
cracking into notes to his children

I leave a string from his door
to my hands,
as if he had always been a dream
of my listening
my head hammers a measure between
his sound
and my straining to stay here,

These Now & Other Poems

in his sleep,
that such a turn again
and again before his piano
could be so silent,
still,
the hammers
never moving.

∾ *Blank Pages*

I need two blank pages to
see one

rough link to sometimes,
blanks and rages

I don't think of me-
                thod
without a body falling
"to the moving floor"

such things strangle in comfort

you tell me things and break silences like frozen
       metal

all
ways surround
"method": the course
a river runs is
not-method but a way, for instance—
a wafer: eat it
& you've eaten it—
put it in your eye and it's in
the way—

but the "river": now *that's* method.
There are ways
to *undo* these things
but not to *do* them.

❦ *For My Father's 70th Birthday*

Even "no one home"
is something there—
an empty house full of
voices or a head
throbbing with noise—
incessant clatter of film
on sprockets
young faces leap out of old light
half of a lens cap
cuts off half of a life
Even the stillness fades
and the soundless piano
swims up into a dream of
aching for a fistful of sentences
that will turn the pounding to prayer—
someone there, in the cropped photographs,
is gone—
a pair of hands
from the edge of the frame
reaches for a child whose adulthood lies
in ambush
Even now,
the odd drifting into memory
shatters like a dropped mirror,
the fragments still staring up from the floor,
wheel upon wheel of still images
scrolled across a hot lamp—
jagged dance of children
—which eyes watch now?—

Michael Blitz

alone in the thin light of a strange room,
looking at the end of one history
and into the inverted focus of a new one—
fathers of sons and daughters give themselves
Even odds that
the children at the door
will knock
or knock it down
just to know if the "no one home"
is over.

∽ And

At the end of the earth
there is an end
to singing
and an ear for a single sound
the "and" comes after
the first whisper and the last
kiss writes the script for the next
last
sound you make
that I hear
as a kiss
but you say it is a word
and a gift
from the ends of the earth
where Mt. Sinai meets Lower Gall Hill
like cool gray bones
and a tangle of braids,
you say it is a word
you cannot say,
you won't allow yourself the fear
of wanting
but the want itself
makes you afraid,
this careful distance you go to say
the end of the world is a phrase,
and an end to wanting,
you can hear the "and" at the beginning
of every sentence
what you say is you want
not to fear the saying,
what you have is the staying

Michael Blitz

afraid of the going,
makes you hear the "and" before the doing
makes you wonder if the distance between
a kiss and the sound of wanting when it fades
is the same as the distance
between your mouth and mine.

∼ "be still my heart…"

beast
'til my heart grinds its bitemarks
into pencils
each day a smaller notebook
fills these sounds with incessant deliberation
The sun sets its rods across my ceiling
vague sound of bees
and cancelled greetings
miles of tape with clicks and starts
a parade of uneasiness
slicks back the necks run through with tapers
the sun lights each wick and disconnects
the day's corset

What do you think it means to be pounding out
the cold metal of
pounding
What do you do with that
pencil
when it makes the sound of
breaking teeth

Still the sun sets the dry heaving shallows into
    old glue
the cool air exceeds itself too big too cool too
    much and what
do you say when your sentences exceed their
    length
the high pitch of rapid forgetting
I swear I will remember every time you tell the
    truth

Michael Blitz

a thousand years of incessant planning for
one shy smile
What do you think to say when you awaken
        distracted by the noise of
bees and hot rain
What do you say to hold something still

Still you are somewhere someone cut out of a
        backdrop
each area is computed as the end of a seizure
each seizure ruptures through the bees and the
        noise
of clicking
fits of lying
too still
the steep pitch
and the buckets of falling down
that stop.

Bus Accident

I shot up into
the mistake of her voice,
I said "is it you?"
She said,
"is it you?"

The windows broke open,
I held out my hands; "how can you be here?"
She held out her hands; "here."

I said, "didn't you die?"
She said, "You die."

I said "Why have you come?"
She said "come."

The air was cold. My eyes were broken.

I said "You can't be real"
She said "Be real."

Her breath and her fingers, cold.
Broken glass on the floor, cold.
The wind in her voice, cold.

I said, "Your dying has killed me."
She said "Killed me."

I said, "There was no time to know you."
She said "No time."

Michael Blitz

I held myself up by meathooks in the wall.

I said, "How do I know it's you"
she said "It's you."

I said, "I can't move."
She said "move"

I broke like a window.
She disappeared.

I said, "Where did you go?"
She said, "I disappeared."

I said "Do you remember the accident?"
She said "I disappeared."

I said, "will I start to forget you?"
She said, "Start to forget."

I said, "Why—?"
She said, "People disappear."

I said, "How can I find you?"
She said, "You disappear."

"What happens now?"
She said, "Don't disappear."

I said, "Don't let me awaken."
She said "awaken."

I shot up in the sound of my voice, broken—

These Now & Other Poems

I said "it was a dream."
She said nothing.

I said, "Was it all a dream?"
She said "All a dream."

"But you're still here?"
She said "still here."

I said nothing.
She said "It's still……
           here."

I said "can you answer me?"
she said "answer me."

I said "can you answer *me*?"
she said "answer *me*."

I said "what are you asking?"
She said, "Was I broken?"

I said, "What are you asking?"
She said "Are you cold?"

I said, "What can you feel?"
She said, "Everything's broken."

I said "will this be the last time?"
She said "What are you asking?."

I said "the last time I'll see you?"
She said "I'll see you."

Michael Blitz

I said "how will I remember you?"
She said "I'll see you."

I said "What will I remember?"
She said "The last time I'll see you."

I said "How long will this time last?"
She said "Remember me."

I said, "Have we said everything?"
She said, "Everything."

I said, "I don't know what to do now."
She said, "Everything."

I said "Can you stay?"
She said "I was broken"

I said, "It's too cold here."
She said, "It's cold here."

I said, "Everything's broken."
She said, "It was an accident."

I said, "But you've come back."
She said, "It was an accident."

I said "Can I go with you?"
She said "People disappear."

~ Day of Rest

sowing plowing reaping binding sheaves threshing winnowing selecting grinding sifting kneading baking shearing wool washing wool beating wool dyeing wool spinning weaving making two loops weaving two threads separating two threads tying untying sewing two stitches tearing trapping slaughtering flaying salting meat curing hide scraping hide cutting hide writing two letters erasing two letters building tearing a building down extinguishing a fire kindling a fire hitting with a hammer taking an object from the private domain to the public or transporting and object in the public domain

what it takes to create a universe,
to build a sanctuary in the wilderness,
to recall the work of the beginning and
to remember the long journey out of bondage—

~ *Thoughts of Everything*

Thoughts of everything,
every day,
thoughts of it, as if
every thought were itself
a day, "itself" a thought,
therefore,
a day of days, everything
a thing thought, therefore
everything every day,
thinking today of this,
therefore, today—everything, thought and
       thinking
at once, two things:
everything and every day,
thinking this, therefore,
all things, not at once:
no "once" but every one day all thoughts,
therefore, no days,
not "days," then but *a* day, now, today,
no more "after *this* or *that*,
therefore no "therefore,"
a day of all things, days, thoughts: thinking this,
therefore no "not thinking"—all days one day,
thinking all days, things, once—not "once" as
       "ago"
(no then unless now), but once as all times,
       things, days, thoughts,
thinkings—thinking "Now" is all "Alls" in one
       "Once,"
one thinks therefore
only one thing
only once.

~ *Footnote*

I spoke to the dancer.
She said, "whattya mean you couldn't tell me from the dance?
I was the one dancing," she said, "The dance was the thing I was doing."

~ *The Instructions*

I have hardly begun—
suddenly, I appear to notice that
I have hardly begun, then
I notice
I *have* begun.

There is an interruption.
I notice I have begun to run,
then I notice that I have nearly run out of time,
and I appear not to be nearly finished,
I interrupt,
having noticed I had nearly begun to run out of
      the room.

I appear not to have noticed the interruption,
and begin to finish,
suddenly running into myself
running back into the room.

I am beginning to notice.

I suddenly appear, running,
in time to begin an interruption.
I notice I am not nearly at the beginning

I appear in the instructions.
Not nearly myself, I hardly notice
I am out of the room.
I am beginning to be finished.

~ **The Simple Truth:**

I will confess nothing
that your eyes have not begged me
to invent.

∾ *Often I Am Permitted Two For One*

kissed under
the crazy white whiteness

BAM father from blanket bed
finds teeth
gloves feet to stairs
calls wife
loads gun bullets
points crazy kiss we two
fall feet to porch door,
where you he say **going damn it**
goes for metal knick knack
click click click he accident dead
whole family
I get lucky get to

kiss her again.

∾ *this side)*

I saw
and I loved that
infinite
fear)

the whip of
recognition
as if the mirror hands
you your fear of being
looked at)

the length of this day becomes a decoration
the tatoo artist forgets himself clear through
to the esophagus
to teach me
that place for these things)

first of
so many
small
places
in which
one can
forget
oneself
in light of
another)

the tatoo, he said,
was to cover "the king"
a green dagger through a skull's eye

Michael Blitz

to hide a blue needle
and tongue)

just inside this perfect
inside I find something
there where nothing was
supposed to keep me even
the stupid has flipped itself
into muteness—mutations in the pain-scape
have left my hands
doing some sort of stupid weeping
no one can read)

this morning sure
it was that dream-sheer
bluffing that
I could stand you
saying it all over again, but this time no
cement mattress covering the door
falling around me in the springs and wires
someone said I made it up
everything I made
I made it
everything
up
I can't believe you
can't you believe I could
make you up,
can't you make it up
for me?)

These Now & Other Poems

it comes down to
bringing it all
up)

we no longer know what punishments
we are)

because she was afraid she wasn't
there)

even the quality of the sadness is a matter
of taste
or that matter, when you ask
what is)

∽ User Friendly

You are in a phone booth and
the wrong number you have dialed can't hear you,
says "hello? hello?" at least ten times before you
    are willing to say
"sorry, wrong number" but it's not that easy.
The wrong number knows that voice from
    somewhere
and now you're not so sure this isn't the one
you were calling, but you can't remember
    exactly,
the noise from outside rubs against the door,
and an odor you know is in the wrong place
creeps up the scratched glass. You are pretty sure
the phone booth's on fire.
The wrong number is yelling something but you
    can't
pay attention, stepping out onto the sidewalk,
    one arm
extended back into the booth, holding the
    phone.
You can feel, more than hear, the wrong number
    screaming
something about a fire
—which interests you
—as does the sweet cool air of the city around
    you,
not a lick of flame, you say "what?"
—the wrong number is yelling, mouth away
    from the phone
—background noise
—crackling…

~ You know that

fine set of fine lies so thin one knows one's
    words only as a
device for tripping into an accident of candor,
& that

any one move presents the conundrum
of all moves— the way one is moved
to tears,
to make the difference between moving and
moving away
count
& that

each time entails one
chance, though
everyone
wants two—

& you know that all lies
rely on an equal mix of truth and desire,

—Not that
lying isn't also praying.

❧ *No Power Is*

No power is practical.
Everything is less a word than the impulse
to slap something
out of someone's hands
or to laugh
until you can make the sound in the back of
    your throat
that drives the turbine out of language.

It takes an ugly power to make an ugly noise.

If you leave right now for Albany, NY,
and if Light leaves when you do,
it will take Light one one-thousandth of a sec-
    ond to arrive at the bridge
across Washington Park Lake, another one-mil-
    lionth of an instant to
flash off the reflecting pool at Rockefeller's Folly,
but you will stop at the thruway hotshop to use
    the bathroom
and to step out of the dark envelope of the first
    two hours,
you will return to your car to find you've left the
    lights on,
or that your flashlight is without batteries,
and the last hour and twenty minutes you will
    ride in silence,
burning calorie upon calorie of loneliness
and the silence will start to kill you.

These Now & Other Poems

There is nothing to say when the batteries are
 dead.
And there is no place to put them that will not
 produce
more darkness.

It takes a lot of candle power to get across the
 street.

Midnight on 87 South,
groaning metal, a Trailways bus on its side,
the rest of the circus animals gathered around,
lights and sirens,
fast hands pulling death from the driver's seat.
No power is big enough to restore that light.
The cops reroute cars and onlookers,
the only real power is forgetfulness.

No power is my permission to substitute sen-
 tences
for the details I wasn't there to see,
this accident, or hers,
relegated to description
and photographs I am grateful I don't have.
Instead, I make a full set of replicas for a
 sequence of events
I know only as afterburn,
it takes a lot of words spooled around aching
 bones
to avoid saying the name of a catastrophe,
when the light flashes WALK,
I am afraid to move.

Michael Blitz

Memory dangles an empty noose.
Every crosswalk fills in the blank
where she had stepped down,
and looked one instant too long into the head-
    lights.
It's taken this long to say death
and mean something the machines can't drown
    out.

For years I have written "you" when I meant
    "I"—
keeping the distance open,
like a phone line,
between the two—
until a crushing silence had become
a hideous vocabulary,

now a tap on the shoulder
is a shudder I miss—
the waitress smiles but hates to listen
the rain snakes through her
thinnest laughter
it takes a noise like her false laughter
to start the breathing again;
it's taken until now to say broken
and hear someone
breaking.
No power is the right power,
my hand has broken things out of sequence
half a lifetime in an overflow of the wrong pro-
    noun,

It has taken too long to get from you to me,
this cup of coffee is a thousand years old,

These Now & Other Poems

My first step across every street takes Light 23
      times around the world,
the time it took for one life to blink out—
my second step takes a lifetime,
takes a lifetime out of me.

Your power is gone only
when I miss it—
otherwise, the noise breaks past you,
or do I mean me?—
I can't stop talking to you when I mean you,
no power is talking through you when I'm lis-
      tening,
It takes a lifetime of listening to hear one word
where there isn't any,
and another to hear exactly the same word a sec-
      ond time,
and I'm listening
like a phone against a sleeping head,
for the one word to restart the turbine,
where no power is practically all there is.

～ Bellows

"her dark hair , in curls, usually circles her
    head"(75)
now red
with sighing
the bread and honey of a new sweet year some-
    one was supposed to promise someone
"but sometimes comes down on one side"(75)
beneath the eyelids like puppets
& a promise to forget
as the gift of sitting still &
of being hungry

[see LINE 23 OF PAGE 77, beginning
with "All right," and ending with "this?"]

"I was willing and receptive but much too
    young" (87)
to follow such a fracture in logic
with anything but an outrageous lack of grace
———too much "like one of those old-time
    Kansas banks that any punk robber could
    knock over"(104/5)

"'I wonder what it is that causes these trou-
    bles'"(108)
"you've singled yourself out as though others
    weren't already giving you plenty of
    heat"(131)
and ice-flakes mingled with a sudden
seriousness,

"this guy is drunk" (307) or just repeating himself
in this or that doorway
one room leads into another problem of simul-
 taneous translation: "I'm talking affective
 phenomena" (316) but leading only to the
 sofa where old toast,
"roots, leaves, stems and flowers" (258) have
 replaced springs and quiet sounds of
"cerebral animalism or primitivism"(242)
or were they the
loud sounds no one can ever be
louder than
—— in what should have been a dream until
 someone else remembered the same thing,
there was no murmurring &
no drone,
the sharp edges embedded in the plaster col-
 lected blood from elbows and shoulders,
a sudden neck upon them,
lips, fingers,
"I stood waiting in the street"(243) but I didn't
 come out &
I had to go back in to look, but
I was already gone
and "we were having one of our typical conver-
 sations"(350) without me——"I apolo-
 gize for these asides. I have to tell the story
 as it happened."(385)
"you take the sexual path and it leads
 you…"(389)
but everything has always been at least
that
& so few

Michael Blitz

know "there's nothing rational"(392) about love
    or its absence,
about the things that lead us
about the hunger that awakens us
"'I wish I could say how'"(413) to live within it
    as I cannot live without it,
but it's the living part,
the living parts
& the tangle of wanting
—or the point may be to have set aside the
    longing ,
to have replaced the absence with distance——
    but "even that
was not remote enough"(442———
"better to thaw *two* hearts"(364)
but that takes
a big fire.

These Now

It was clear that she and I were better off for parting and that aching is part of the beauty of the world.

[Kevin Patterson, The Water in Between]

∾ *These Now*

These things
nearly
written will think
I have been
what happened—

These Now & Other Poems

trying to learn
photographs
what they
knew

Michael Blitz

gone to see her
to live

These Now & Other Poems

in the end
few words of
no mention of

Michael Blitz

I saw that she was
her tears were
violent scenes
I should have
realized what she
offered

These Now & Other Poems

the time
she

someone wakened

Michael Blitz

over
and over
she was
something

These Now & Other Poems

this statement: "I
am there

Michael Blitz

nothing
but the
want
—but need
heavily

These Now & Other Poems

exactness of the
something more
and the only
accurate details

Michael Blitz

events seem to
allow
no one

These Now & Other Poems

say to me,
"I
was tormented
by
effort   silence
that effort

Michael Blitz

that
conversation
was no longer an
enemy

These Now & Other Poems

breathe,
coughing
all that extravagant
perfectly beautiful
expression
of her eyes

eyes   almost

Michael Blitz

her
gaze
　　was
spent
　　about her

These Now & Other Poems

able to stand
absent
she
went there
   and now
out

Michael Blitz

     I had
       to live
and she had

    she had
This.

These Now & Other Poems

```
            the
     moment
              gone
all
sightless
```

Michael Blitz

an instant
over her, I
—a sort of breath
      opened

These Now & Other Poems

uneasy
something
linked to me

strange as
distinct thought

Michael Blitz

I would have
written to me
but not
the memory

These Now & Other Poems

near the end
one shouldn't
want to come in
all the more

Michael Blitz

as I did,
at that moment,
she might

These Now & Other Poems

her
continuing
rattle
to point to

Michael Blitz

dazzling
such
an extraordinary
    illness
she was still in

These Now & Other Poems

thought

    it

time

Michael Blitz

                    I
would have believed
what I   say

could return to

These Now & Other Poems

for a moment
rasping breath

come early, she said

Michael Blitz

altogether
penetrating
(she remained)
two or three
irregular beat

These Now & Other Poems

    exactly

demands a
thousand times

Michael Blitz

understand this

    everyone

astonishes me

    that is itself

These Now & Other Poems

the
answer
in
not
on her

Michael Blitz

it would occur
beautiful
she
perfectly
made everything

These Now & Other Poems

history
amounted to a
forgetting
rather delicate

Michael Blitz

a kind of
difficulty
    forgetting
very clearly
before
I had to
her/this ride on the
great sadness

These Now & Other Poems

secret
having
the place
it is a
who

Michael Blitz

anything else
she had
so faint
just enough

These Now & Other Poems

        into
     the noise
arrow

toward the

         angry
I don't know

Michael Blitz

   as someone
      complete
  throwing
entirely
       her
      not
  her
   which
her   herself

These Now & Other Poems

the immense task of
              her

       intimacy

Michael Blitz

      days
      I
could not remember
    the door

These Now & Other Poems

sometimes

the only thing
			to feel

	she said
	she
	was proof

Michael Blitz

into the
difficulty
everything
reserved appearance

These Now & Other Poems

    I am talking
and I am ignoring

the hours
are dead

refuge in it

Michael Blitz

        sleep
     broke
my lips

These Now & Other Poems

these things
I *did*
not I *was*

true for
people & objects

Michael Blitz

                the
violent
sadness of
one second

dispossessed

These Now & Other Poems

in the shape of her

far away
but still

    here

Michael Blitz

she cries
the asylum

These Now & Other Poems

she answered
more exact
the one story
I was

Michael Blitz

yes

became
to tremble

These Now & Other Poems

        poison
              sort
      of empty
     that room
    it was
doors

Michael Blitz

wanted her
    movement
that
    animal
irritation

These Now & Other Poems

corridors of

that
agitation

Michael Blitz

because she was

    I went

anyone would

These Now & Other Poems

for example
neither ear, nor
thought
keep her away
    I'm going over
to see

Michael Blitz

she was home
it happened

These Now & Other Poems

more to
   happen

Michael Blitz

    her

        language

   language
          unknown
          form of
          have

These Now & Other Poems

the
language of someone

the more I wanted

Michael Blitz

that I

    touched her
something was being

hurled

These Now & Other Poems

went
hot   next

quite tranquil
not
working
on a sort of
cold
I always carried

Michael Blitz

a sudden pressing up against
everything
carried me
the world could
breathe

These Now & Other Poems

      (that)
 (one)
   (force)
(the)
     (certainty)
(to find)
   (her   there

Michael Blitz

the dark
hand

that hand.

These Now & Other Poems

these bodies
so intense
not a
depth
the outside
seems to have

Michael Blitz

watched her
thinking

the
    term
of uneasiness

These Now & Other Poems

her

    and her

        fact

Michael Blitz

       I talk
driven to talk
to form
the space
          her
physical certainty

heads and hands.

She shook.

Michael Blitz

"I thought
you up in this room"

her hand, that
accord

These Now & Other Poems

but she was
   sudden
her contact

no longer
the word
the memory of

Michael Blitz

   A form of
thought
or its victim
equal to
absence
in the face

These Now & Other Poems

face of something
I've known all along
exactly

Michael Blitz

and besides
    the real,
  my
secrecy about this
whole day

0-595-21552-1